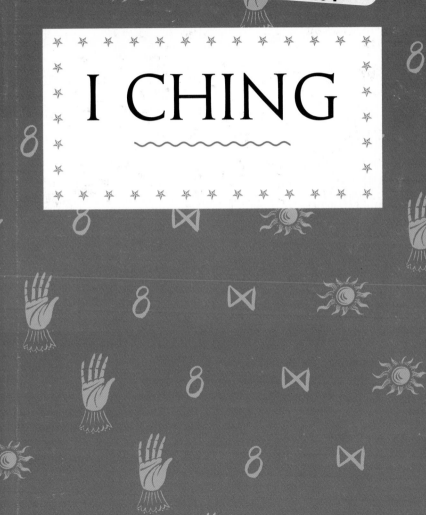

# I CHING

# I CHING

## MARY CLARK

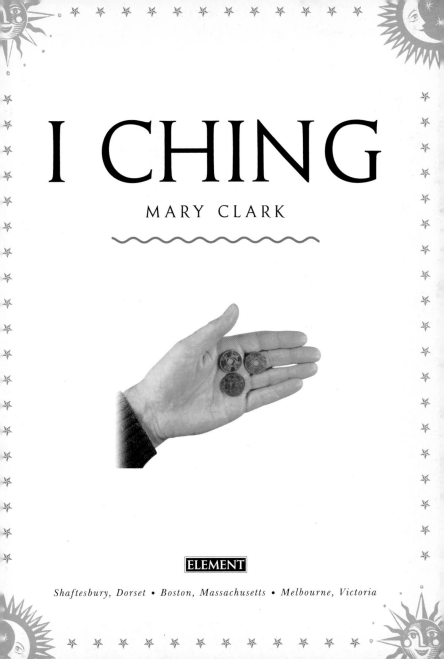

**ELEMENT**

*Shaftesbury, Dorset • Boston, Massachusetts • Melbourne, Victoria*

© Element Books Limited 1998

First published in Great Britain in 1998 by
ELEMENT BOOKS LIMITED
Shaftesbury, Dorset SP7 8BP

Published in the USA in 1998 by
ELEMENT BOOKS INC.
160 North Washington Street, Boston, MA 02114

Published in Australia in 1998 by
ELEMENT BOOKS
and distributed by Penguin Australia Ltd
487 Maroondah Highway, Ringwood, Victoria 3134

Designed and created with
The Bridgewater Book Company

Printed and bound in Italy by Graphicom S.r.l.

British Library Cataloguing in Publication data available

Library of Congress Cataloging in Publication data available

ISBN: 1 86204 265 9

ELEMENT BOOKS LIMITED
Editorial Director *Julia McCutchen*
Senior Commissioning Editor *Caro Ness*
Managing Editor *Miranda Spicer*
Production Director *Roger Lane*
Production *Sarah Golden*

THE BRIDGEWATER BOOK COMPANY
Art Director *Peter Bridgewater*
Designer *Stephen Parker*
Managing Editor *Anne Townley*
Project Editor *Caroline Earle*
Picture Research *Vanessa Fletcher*
Three Dimensional Models *Mark Jamieson*
Location Photography *Karen Hatch*

Picture credits:
e.t. archive, Images Colour Library, and Stock Market.

# CONTENTS

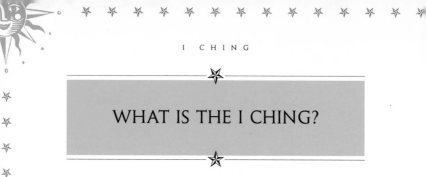

# WHAT IS THE I CHING?

*The I Ching (pronounced "ee cheeng") is a book of divination, of symbols to provide insight into life, relationships, health, wealth, and happiness. The I Ching is the ancient Chinese Book of Changes, which gives the user an insight into the forces, literally "the changes," that are occurring at any particular moment in time.*

## PATTERNS OF LIFE

In the West, patterns seen in natural things were used as indicators of immediate conditions in the flow of events in time. In China, the patterns that diviners saw in nature were standardized and related to a book of readings – the I Ching – thereby putting these patterns into a formal framework that can be used as easily today as it was thousands of years ago.

This book was originally written to keep people in touch with the flow of universal life energy and the information buried in the unconscious. A person who consults the I Ching can expect to receive insights into the hidden energies and tendencies underlying the situation in question. The purpose of the oracle is to remind us that we are part of a bigger picture. Our concerns cannot be separated from the flow of life around us. By gaining insight into the larger patterns surrounding us, we can choose the path of least effort and greatest delight.

*The I Ching is a powerful tool that is easy to use. You do not need to have psychic powers. The oracle can be accessed by tossing three coins and reading their pattern of heads and tails.*

The I Ching consists of a set of 64 hexagrams, or six-lined figures. Each hexagram has a name and a set of words or phrases that describe it. You can consult the I Ching whenever you want more information about a part of your life. You need simply to focus your thoughts into a question, and follow the instructions for building a hexagram – the six-lined figure central to interpretation of the I Ching. Then look up the meaning of the hexagram for insight into your question. For over 3,000 years, the Chinese have consulted the wisdom of the I Ching to find a balanced way through life's tribulations.

*Divination methods have been used over thousands of years. The Vikings developed runes, a set of symbolic stones; astrology has been used by the Egyptians, Greeks, Chinese, and Indians.*

THE CHINESE DREW YARROW STALKS TO CONSULT THE I CHING.

## A SHORT HISTORY

周易 The words found in the I Ching are older than the book itself and come from a special shamanic language of ancient China. At the heart of Chinese philosophy lies the concept that all things are created from a mixture of opposites: yin (feminine, heavy, earth, yielding) and yang (masculine, light, heaven, active). Yang is represented by a single straight line, yin by a single line divided in half.

YIN          YANG

These lines eventually became structured into the hexagrams. About 3,000 years ago, Wu Hsien put together a way to access the information in the hexagrams by counting yarrow stalks. This book and method, then called the Chou I, was used by the kings of the Chou dynasty to overthrow their enemies and establish peace. Their descendants continued to use the Chou I to keep in touch with the Tao, or the path of energy flow in every being and situation.

*The I Ching has been consulted by royalty and common folk in China for over 3,000 years.*

For its first 500 years, the Chou I was essentially an oracle of kings. People outside the ruling class began to consult the Chou I during the Warring States period. At that time, society was beginning to fall apart, and more and more people sought guidance on how to respond to the massive political and social change. Since then, the oracle has continued to guide people from all walks of life.

In about 200 B.C.E., at the start of the Han dynasty, scholars compiled all existing versions of the Chou I and made it into a Ching, or a classic text. That classic compilation, or I Ching, is essentially the same text we know today.

THE YIN/YANG SYMBOL IS AT THE CENTER OF CHINESE PHILOSOPHY.

Images and phrases from the I Ching have been used in poetry, politics, and literature. References to this ancient Chinese text can commonly be found throughout the whole of Chinese culture, and the book is still used as an oracle by those wishing to follow the natural path of the Tao.

*I Ching is most often translated as Book of Changes. While this translation is accurate, it is not complete. "Ching" refers not just to a book, but to a classic – a work prized by generations, fundamental to a civilization. "I" refers to changes in the flow of life energy: whether it is on the rise or is declining.*

## THE TAOIST VIEW OF LIFE

The word Tao is commonly translated as way or path. But its meaning goes far beyond those everyday words. In his philosophical classic *Tao Te Ching*, or *The Way of Change*, Lao Tsu wrote, "The Tao that can be spoken of is not the real (eternal) Tao." He writes of the Tao as a sense of order, a recognition of the growth cycles in all things, and he advocates flowing with the changes, not against them.

LAO TSU, LEGENDARY FOUNDER OF TAOISM.

The concept of the changing universe comes from the basic nature of yin and yang. When yang is in force too long, it grows weak and becomes yin. The yielding yin gains power in rest and becomes active yang. In life, a yin situation can be acted upon with dynamic action. To use force in a situation that is already yang would lead to "butting heads" with the yang energy – force against force. Far better to yield to the prevailing yang and gain from its power.

To the Taoists, life was not to be acted upon, but joined with. We should work with rather than against the natural order of the world. The purpose of our lives is not discovered by being alone, but by finding which ways flow best with the prevailing energy state at any given time. The benefits of learning to live close to the Tao are not riches, or worldly gain, but Te, or the ability to manifest Tao in action.

*To be connected to the Tao, or "natural law," means to experience effortlessness and delight as we take the next step on the path we have chosen – or the path that has chosen us.*

## THE FUNCTION OF THE I CHING HEXAGRAM

Fu Hsi, an early sage, recognized that the eight basic elements of the universe could be described as a combination of three divided yin or undivided yang lines. These elemental trigrams are named after the element they represent: Heaven, Earth, Thunder, Water, Mountain, Wind, Fire, and Lake.

Some time around 1123 B.C.E., King Wen of the state of Zhou stacked the trigrams on top of each other, creating hexagrams, or six-lined figures. There are 64 possible combinations of the eight trigrams, and Wen wrote 64 short paragraphs explaining each of them. These hexagrams further illustrate the concept of the changing Tao through the interrelation of the trigram elements: Heaven stacked over Fire (Heaven/Fire), Earth yielding to Thunder (Thunder/Earth). For purposes of divination, the combination of yin and yang represented by the elements in the hexagram, and their relative position, top or bottom, created a metaphorical picture of the elements at work in one's own life situation.

FU HSI, THE SEMI-MYTHICAL SHAMAN, WHO DEVISED
THE EIGHT BASIC TRIGRAMS OF THE I CHING.

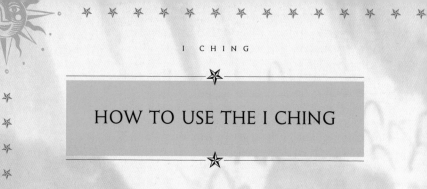

# HOW TO USE THE I CHING

*Before you can find an answer, you must have a question. As simplistic as this may sound, it is crucial to a successful interpretation of the hexagram. The clearer you can be in your questioning, the more the I Ching can tell you about the answer.*

BEFORE YOU BEGIN TO CONSULT THE I CHING, MAKE SURE YOU HAVE A CLEAR QUESTION TO ASK.

## THE QUESTION

周易 Ask the oracle any question. You might want to ask about a current relationship. A general question such as, "What's happening in my relationship with – ?" would probably yield a very general hexagram, and it might be hard to tell if the hexagram referred to a large underlying pattern or day-to-day ups and downs. If you were to ask "What is the likelihood for a mutually fulfilling long-term relationship with – ?" you have specified the particular area of information you wish to pinpoint and the hexagram will provide a more detailed answer.

Learning the answer to one specific question might raise more questions in your mind. Ask as many questions as you wish. Let the information from the hexagrams guide you to new questions as you uncover the hidden tendencies in your situation.

*There is no limit to the amount of questions you can ask the I Ching at any given time. Let the information from the hexagram lead you to ask further, more specific questions.*

## TECHNIQUES TO BUILD A HEXAGRAM

周易 Techniques for casting a hexagram reveal the makeup of the elements that form the hexagram line by line, starting at the bottom. The two most popular methods for determining the order of yin and yang lines are throwing coins or yarrow stalks. You should ideally work at a table, or on a flat surface. You'll need a pen and a piece of paper to record your lines.

Three thousand years ago, when Wu Hsien first devised a way to access the I Ching, he developed a complicated system of mathematical steps in dividing bunches of sticks or yarrow stalks. The process could take up to a half hour to complete. While there are still some people who use this method, most people today cast a hexagram using a very simple process of throwing coins.

It is important to read descriptions of both hexagrams if you have had any changing lines (*see* p.47). The more changing lines, the more drastic and far reaching the change. A situation with no changing lines is solidly represented by the description of the hexagram, with no change for the near future.

## THE LINE POSITIONS

These are the fundamental building blocks of the I Ching. They are distinguished by their quality – yin or yang – as well as by their position. Historically each line position has a special significance.

Because a hexagram is built from the bottom up, the changing first line indicates a fundamental problem or change, something that cannot find a solid foundation. The changing second line reveals instability. The third line often points to change due to unforeseen timing shifts. The fourth line can indicate changes due to other people's involvement. The fifth line is a beneficent line, and can point to changes because of unforeseen advancement. The sixth line points to a situation that is overbalanced – it will be over before it has begun.

*The most important line position is the position of the changing line or lines.*

For an in-depth understanding of the meaning of a particular line position in a given hexagram, refer to the list of books for suggested further reading (*see* p. 55).

## THE IMPORTANCE OF THE CHANGING LINE

Just as the combination of elements in a hexagram creates a dynamic (Wind/Mountain), the elements themselves are changing into each other. When yang is powerful for too long, it yields to yin. If any line in a hexagram changes from yang to yin or yin to yang, a new hexagram is formed. Thus an I Ching reading can produce one static hexagram to describe a stable situation or two hexagrams, one that is changing into another, for situations in flux.

*Changing lines show that the situation is shifting. Use the information from both hexagrams to see how you can direct the change toward your desired outcome.*

## KEY TO THE HEXAGRAM NUMBERS

Use the hexagram chart (*see* p.54) to locate the number of your hexagram. Find the lower and upper trigrams, and follow the chart to find the number of the hexagram they form.

# THE MEANING OF THE 64 HEXAGRAMS

*The following pages detail the meaning of the 64 hexagrams. Each hexagram is a combination of two trigrams, and the eight trigram elements represent different kinds of spirit power. The hexagram you cast will indicate how each of these elements is interacting.*

## KEY TO THE ELEMENTS

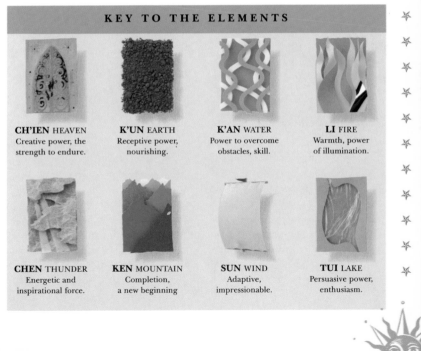

**CH'IEN** HEAVEN
Creative power, the
strength to endure.

**K'UN** EARTH
Receptive power,
nourishing.

**K'AN** WATER
Power to overcome
obstacles, skill.

**LI** FIRE
Warmth, power
of illumination.

**CHEN** THUNDER
Energetic and
inspirational force.

**KEN** MOUNTAIN
Completion,
a new beginning

**SUN** WIND
Adaptive,
impressionable.

**TUI** LAKE
Persuasive power,
enthusiasm.

## 1. CH'IEN HEAVEN / HEAVEN
## CREATIVE FORCE IN ACTION

KEYWORDS
*♦ dynamic ♦ enduring ♦ moving ♦*
*♦ energy ♦ the sun ♦*

## 2. K'UN EARTH / EARTH
## NURTURING RECEPTIVITY

KEYWORDS
*♦ nourishing ♦ serving ♦ receptive ♦*
*♦ power ♦ the earth ♦*

The great force of heaven is the beginning of all things, and this power is available to you now. Persistence is the key to access the creative force. If you remain true to your vision, you will flow with perfect timing in your endeavor. This hexagram inspires, transforms, and brings harmony to every situation.

In all situations, your path is to support and not to lead. Be of service in any way possible, and bring to all things a sense of balance and peace. Provide each situation with what it needs without judgment. Allow yourself a time of quiet reflection and contemplation to recharge your energy. Yield gracefully to the decisions and plans of others.

## 3. CHUN WATER / THUNDER
### INCUBATION

> KEYWORDS
> ✦ planting ✦ accumulating ✦
> ✦ difficult ✦ beginning ✦

## 4. MENG MOUNTAIN / WATER
### INEXPERIENCE

> KEYWORDS
> ✦ unaware ✦ young ✦
> ✦ closed or covered ✦

MOUNTAIN

WATER

Do not expect things to proceed quickly and easily. If you expect the worst, you will be pleasantly surprised by the outcome. Give things space to grow by themselves. Occupy yourself with other projects while this situation incubates. Once things get going, the situation will prove to be abundantly fruitful and stimulating.

Your inexperience clouds your understanding – you are unaware of the true nature of the situation at hand. Stay on the sidelines and gather information. Be aware of your inexperience and seek to learn from others. Don't pretend to understand outside events and do not act prematurely. By increasing your knowledge you increase your chances for success.

## 5. HSÜ WATER / HEAVEN
## WAITING

> **KEYWORDS**
> ◆ *hesitate* ◆ *have patience* ◆
> ◆ *stopped by rain* ◆

## 6. SUNG HEAVEN / WATER
## CONFLICT

> **KEYWORDS**
> ◆ *quarrels* ◆ *controversy* ◆
> ◆ *seeking justice* ◆

HEAVEN

WATER

Patience is the keyword here, because now it is time to wait. Timing is of the utmost importance, and you must carefully observe your situation, waiting on the right moment to advance your projects or make a move. Don't worry, though, for when the time comes to act you will have no doubts. Be patient and wait for now.

Confrontation surrounds you. Clarify your viewpoint as best you can without arousing more conflict. Remain neutral if possible, or avoid the situation entirely. Don't try to fulfill your plans in the midst of conflict and do not attempt to influence those around you. Be aware that the conflict may be inside yourself.

**7. SHIH** EARTH / WATER
## LEADERSHIP

> KEYWORDS
> ♦ *discipline* ♦ *organization* ♦
> ♦ *imitate a master* ♦

**8. PI** WATER / EARTH
## GROUPING

> KEYWORDS
> ♦ *harmonize* ♦ *unite* ♦
> ♦ *create with a new center* ♦

WATER

EARTH

Everything around you is confused. This is your opportunity to take the lead. Pay attention to detail, and apply yourself to organizing all aspects of your endeavor. Model yourself after people you admire. Surround yourself with people to whom you can delegate, and offer them a leader's support and encouragement.

Look at the underlying reasons that have created your current situation. What ideals or principles are shared by those around you? It's time to address the fundamental principles of your life. Reorganize all aspects of your affairs according to new ideals. You've outgrown your current situation.

## 9. HSIAO CH'U WIND / HEAVEN
## SMALL GATHERING

> KEYWORDS
> ✦ *take in* ✦ *tolerate* ✦
> ✦ *tame or train animals* ✦

WIND

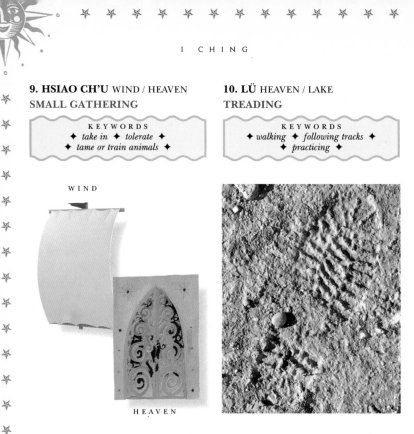

HEAVEN

You are surrounded by seemingly unrelated details. Pay attention to each bit of information and store it for the future. The overlying pattern is invisible at this time. By gathering as much information as possible, you are placing yourself in the strongest position, which may result in ultimate success. Use this time to gain expertise.

## 10. LÜ HEAVEN / LAKE
## TREADING

> KEYWORDS
> ✦ *walking* ✦ *following tracks* ✦
> ✦ *practicing* ✦

Tread carefully. Do not plan too far ahead, but take everything one step at a time. The sequence of events you initiate is of great importance. The path is there, but difficult. Gain practice by proceeding step by step. Pause after each step to check your position and adjust your path. Through this you will achieve your goal.

**11. T'AI** EARTH / HEAVEN
**PEACEFUL FLOW**

KEYWORDS
✦ *prosperous* ✦ *fertile* ✦ *great* ✦

**12. P'I** HEAVEN / EARTH
**OBSTRUCTION**

KEYWORDS
✦ *obstacle* ✦ *disapproval* ✦
✦ *keep quiet* ✦

EARTH

HEAVEN

You are flowing with spirit and able to channel peace and prosperity to all. Share your abundance, spread the spirit of peace to all you meet. In this way you continue the flow of spirit through you and learn how to remain connected to your source in a variety of situations. Enjoy this blessed time.

You are blocked at every turn. Do not attempt to proceed in this situation, and do not try to impose your will. You will only lose by continuing along this path. You must accept that there is an obstacle to your plans and seek the first opportunity to leave quietly. Wait patiently and you will find a fresh field for your endeavor.

## 13. T'UNG JEN HEAVEN / FIRE
### FRIENDSHIP

KEYWORDS
✦ community ✦ sharing ✦
✦ agreement ✦

## 14. TA YU FIRE / HEAVEN
### PROSPERITY

KEYWORDS
✦ goal orientation ✦ nobility ✦
✦ possessions ✦

FIRE

HEAVEN

Join with those who share your vision and can help achieve your goals. This concern is of great benefit to all. Develop friendship and nurture common bonds of understanding. Find the means to unite everyone involved in the spirit of the common good. Bring warmth and enthusiasm to your close friendships.

Through persistence and the desire to improve things, you have found the key to abundance. By firmly committing to your goals you now have the ability to gain financially, creatively, emotionally, and spiritually. Be generous with your new wealth and keep the flow coming to you by sharing with others.

## 15. CH'IEN EARTH / MOUNTAIN
## HUMILITY

KEYWORDS
♦ *yielding* ♦ *simplicity* ♦ *courtesy* ♦

EARTH

MOUNTAIN

## 16. YÜ THUNDER / EARTH
## PREPARING

KEYWORDS
♦ *precautions* ♦ *contentment* ♦
♦ *rejoicing* ♦

The situation is complicated, and your ego may be involved. Simplicity and humility are the keys to success. Reexamine the fundamental issues, and find the simplest possible solution. Be modest about your part in the process. Reduce any clutter, stick with the essentials.

You are in a holding pattern. While waiting for the green light from the universe, take time now to prepare for any future eventualities. Accumulate resources that could be of use once your plans are in full flower. Think things through several times so that you can relax and flow smoothly with events when the timing is right.

## 17. SUI LAKE / THUNDER
## FOLLOWING

KEYWORDS
✦ on a path ✦ in sequence ✦
✦ inevitable ✦

## 18. KU MOUNTAIN / WIND
## ERROR

KEYWORDS
✦ poisoning ✦ seduction ✦
✦ evil spells ✦

MOUNTAIN

WIND

The universe is preparing a path for you. All that is necessary is that you follow it. Flow in the direction things are already heading. Take the path of least resistance. Submit your own will to follow the direction that effortlessly appears. This is your assignment from the universe.

You are in a situation in which you've built on a corrupt foundation, and must now stop for repairs. Seek out miscommunications and deviant viewpoints, either to set them straight or to jettison them altogether. Once you have cleaned up confusion and error, be sure to wait patiently for a new path to emerge. Your increased success will be worth the wait.

**19. LIN** EARTH / LAKE
**APPROACHING**

> KEYWORDS
> ◆ inspect ◆ approve of ◆ honor ◆

**20. KUAN** (WIND / EARTH)
**CONTEMPLATION**

> KEYWORDS
> ◆ examination ◆ instruction ◆
> ◆ an observatory ◆

WIND

EARTH

You are on the verge of attaining a higher level: creatively, spiritually, and emotionally. Don't rush the process or try to impose your vision, but let greatness approach you in its own time. Keep your expectations humble, and enjoy each rung of the ladder as you climb to the top.

In the midst of striving, you have lost sight of the big picture. Step back and observe all aspects of your situation. Take time to contemplate the possible actions available to you. Direct your attention in particular to any area you avoid thinking about, for in detached contemplation you can find a simple solution.

## 21. SHIH HO FIRE / THUNDER
### GNAWING

KEYWORDS
✦ bite ✦ crush ✦ arrive at truth ✦

## 22. PI MOUNTAIN / FIRE
### BEAUTIFY

KEYWORDS
✦ outward appearance ✦ display ✦
✦ passion ✦

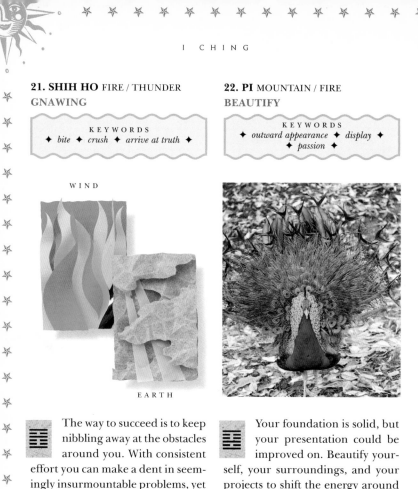

WIND

EARTH

The way to succeed is to keep nibbling away at the obstacles around you. With consistent effort you can make a dent in seemingly insurmountable problems, yet your activity can be small enough to go unnoticed by those who would see you fail. Be sure to pay close attention to your detractors, and do not hesitate to instigate legal action in order to protect yourself.

Your foundation is solid, but your presentation could be improved on. Beautify yourself, your surroundings, and your projects to shift the energy around you. Show off your gifts, be dazzling and delightful; this will increase your value in the eyes of the world and show those who can help you that you are ready to move on.

**23. PO** MOUNTAIN / EARTH
**PRUNING**

KEYWORDS
✦ remove ✦ uncover ✦ cut away ✦

**24. FU** EARTH / THUNDER
**RETURN**

KEYWORDS
✦ renew ✦ retrace ✦ rebirth ✦

EARTH

THUNDER

You are overloaded with information, contacts, and complications. Strip away all useless parts of your endeavor. Pare down to the essentials to improve your chances for success. You will be amazed at how light your load will become, and how swiftly you are carried to fertile fields of success.

You've made good headway but have lost contact with your original inspiration. Go back to your source, the idea or vision that gave birth to your present condition. Returning to the source of this vision will reconnect you to the stream of effortless energy and restimulate contact with helpful people.

## 25. WU WANG HEAVEN / THUNDER
## DISENTANGLING

KEYWORDS
♦ rash ♦ reckless ♦ enmeshed ♦

In order to advance, you must look deep into your motives. Emotional attachments such as pride, greed, obsession, vanity, or revenge must be released because they are preventing you from responding to new information about your goal. If you do not let go of negative emotion, you will remain entangled, and lose your chance of success.

## 26. TA CH'U MOUNTAIN / HEAVEN
## FOCUSED ACTIVITY

KEYWORDS
♦ leadership ability ♦ control ♦
♦ raising to greatness ♦

MOUNTAIN

HEAVEN

You can determine what has value by focusing on a central idea, and relating all things to it. Once you have focus, get moving, and test your ideas in the outside world. You have potential for greatness. This is the right time to initiate big plans.

## 27. YI MOUNTAIN / THUNDER
## NOURISHMENT

KEYWORDS
♦ eat ♦ take in ♦ provide necessities ♦

Now is the time to assess the way your actions are feeding you mentally, emotionally, physically, and spiritually. Are you feeding yourself what you need? This applies to literal food as well as ideas, friends, surroundings, and work. Look at what is nourishing to others, and do what you can to provide it. Be around others who nurture you.

## 28. TA KUO LAKE / WIND
## CRISIS

KEYWORDS
♦ greatness ♦ surpassing ♦
♦ getting clear of ♦

LAKE

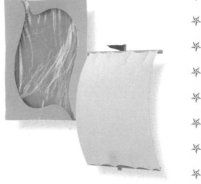

WIND

The going is tough, but this is your opportunity to shine under pressure. Your foundations are unstable. Decide what is most important to you, then act swiftly and with confidence to re-establish your grounding and support. Be open to new information in rebuilding for the future.

### 29. K'AN WATER / WATER
### TRAINING

KEYWORDS
✦ *coaching* ✦ *repetition* ✦ *skill* ✦

You are on the verge of an overwhelming situation, but there is no way out except by going through it. You have the opportunity to practice overcoming obstacles by being faced with them frequently. The keyword at this time is practice – you gain strength by repeating actions until you succeed. Let go of the outcome and practice the daily process of overcoming the obstacles to your vision.

### 30. LI FIRE / FIRE
### ILLUMINATING

KEYWORDS
✦ *brightness* ✦ *warmth* ✦
✦ *articulation* ✦

It is time to spread your light to others – to clarify your needs and goals, illuminate new paths, and bring warmth through personal contact. Use this time of illumination internally, by making conscious your inner motives and needs. Be open to unexpected contact and new possibilities – your power of illumination to discern the benefits and limitations of every new contact

## 31. HSIEN LAKE / MOUNTAIN
### UNITING

KEYWORDS
♦ contact ♦ wholeness ♦
♦ mobilization ♦

## 32. HENG THUNDER / WIND
### CONSISTENCY

KEYWORDS
♦ enduring ♦ habitual ♦
♦ the cycles of the moon ♦

LAKE

THUNDER

MOUNTAIN

WIND

Your focus, energy, or information is scattered. Now is the time to bring together that which belongs together. Be open to anything that influences you or triggers you to action. Reach out and join with others. Someone or something has a vital piece of the puzzle that you need.

This hexagram represents persistence – a consistent application of effort and intention toward a goal. Success in your endeavor depends on your ability to persevere in spite of any obstacles to your goal. You need not wear yourself out by giving everything at all times – your steps can be small and comfortable as long as they are consistent.

## 33. TUN HEAVEN / MOUNTAIN
## WITHDRAWAL

KEYWORDS
✦ obscurity ✦ seclusion ✦ trickster ✦

## 34. TA CHUANG THUNDER / HEAVEN
## WITHDRAWAL POWERFUL

KEYWORDS
✦ inspiration ✦ nobility ✦ maturity ✦

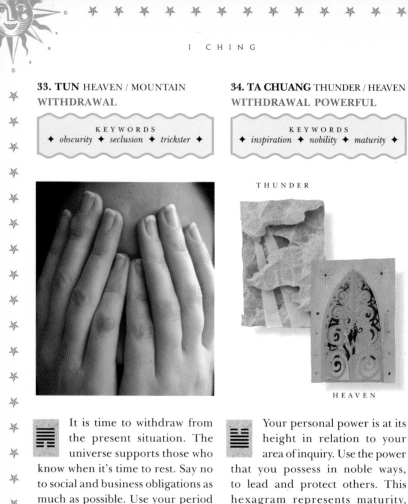

THUNDER

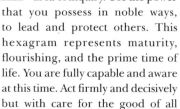

HEAVEN

It is time to withdraw from the present situation. The universe supports those who know when it's time to rest. Say no to social and business obligations as much as possible. Use your period of rest and retreat to rebuild your strength. Avoid difficult people.

Your personal power is at its height in relation to your area of inquiry. Use the power that you possess in noble ways, to lead and protect others. This hexagram represents maturity, flourishing, and the prime time of life. You are fully capable and aware at this time. Act firmly and decisively but with care for the good of all around you.

## 35. CHIN FIRE / EARTH
### FLOURISHING

KEYWORDS
◆ rise ◆ permeate ◆ a promotion ◆

## 36. MING YI EARTH / FIRE
### DARKNESS

KEYWORDS
◆ consciousness ◆ awareness ◆
◆ uncouth people ◆

EARTH

FIRE

The sun is coming out from behind the clouds. Step into the light and enjoy the beauty around you. Be enthusiastic, share what you have, and encourage others to relax and smell the flowers. Your calm strength and easy flowing ways will attract others and your affairs will prosper.

You are swimming in uncertain waters. Voluntarily dim your own brightness and conceal your strengths. Continue to work, but draw no attention to yourself. This will enable you to assess the dangers that lie ahead and render them harmless. Conceal yourself in the darkness.

## 37. CHIA JEN WIND / FIRE
### FAMILY

> KEYWORDS
> ◆ relations ◆ community ◆
> ◆ mastery of a skill ◆

WIND

FIRE

## 38. K'UEI FIRE / LAKE
### SEPARATION

> KEYWORDS
> ◆ contrary ◆ creative tension ◆
> ◆ an odd perspective ◆

Your strength comes from the nurturing group of people around you. Focus on improving the quality of your relationships with others – at work, at home, and socially. Support others with warmth, sincerity, and enthusiasm. Focus your energies on bringing out the best in people. Relax and enjoy the peaceful home you have created.

You are separated from your desired result. Now you can learn the way that opposites (earth/water, man/woman, teacher/student) work together. Clarify what is working against you while acknowledging an underlying connection. Adjust small details to work with the power of the opposition. Acknowledge and use the power of the opposite as your own.

## 39. CHIEN WATER / MOUNTAIN
### OBSTACLES

KEYWORDS
✦ *crooked* ✦ *poverty* ✦ *pride* ✦

## 40. HSIEH THUNDER / WATER
### LOOSENING

KEYWORDS
✦ *discharge* ✦ *free from constraint* ✦
✦ *sever* ✦

THUNDER

WATER

Your path is rocky, but your biggest obstacle is your attitude. Refuse to criticize your situation. Don't dwell on the past or on others' success, but renew your mind with positive thoughts. Surround yourself with uplifting people and ideas. Your negative thinking is blocking your own way.

Just as a thunderstorm clears the tension in the air, you can take action at this time to dispel tensions. Stir things up, pardon or forgive, solve problems, analyze, then take swift action. Untie yourself from troubling situations. This brings a flood of support from the universe.

## 41. SUN MOUNTAIN / LAKE
### DECREASE

> KEYWORDS
> ✦ give away ✦ lessen ✦
> ✦ a sacrificial offering ✦

## 42. YI WIND / THUNDER
### INCREASE

> KEYWORDS
> ✦ benefits ✦ profit ✦ overflowing ✦

WIND

THUNDER

Clean out your closets, your drawers, and your ideas. Get rid of anything or anyone who is not serving your higher purpose. Fearlessly assess your own habits and attitudes. Ask yourself, "Why am I doing what I am doing?" Consciously make room for anything that is new in your life.

This is a time of abundance, a fertile period of harvesting the profits of your labors. You have great power at this moment, so don't rest – use your skill to continue increasing while you are in the flow. Move forward, implement plans, continue to build on your endeavors. Let your overflow stimulate those around you to greater productivity.

## 43. KUAI LAKE / HEAVEN
### DETERMINATION

> KEYWORDS
> ♦ resolution ♦ settlement ♦
> ♦ cleaning a wound ♦

LAKE

HEAVEN

Misperceptions and errors are building up around you. It is time to state your purpose in clear and certain terms. Resolve to confront any difficulties headlong, without force or undue negativity. Keep expressing your position in the face of opposition. The universal forces will support your words if you are showing sufficient determination.

## 44. KOU HEAVEN / WIND
### ATTRACTION

> KEYWORDS
> ♦ magnetism ♦ chance encounters ♦
> ♦ primal forces ♦

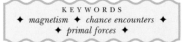

This is a time to be open to the unknown. A brief meeting can lead to new possibilities. You are moved by attraction. Let yourself be drawn to things, respond with truth to what you find enticing. Enjoy the surge of energy that attraction brings, but do not form attachments at this time. This time is a period of change and will not last. Use the energy to replenish yourself, not to lay new foundations.

## 45. TS'UI LAKE / EARTH
### GATHERING

KEYWORDS
✦ unity ✦ concentration ✦
✦ a team of animals ✦

## 46. SHENG EARTH / WIND
### ASCENDING

KEYWORDS
✦ promotion ✦ effort ✦
✦ fulfilled potential ✦

EARTH

WIND

Your leadership powers are strong now. Use them to gather support. Inspire others with your vision. Seek out powerful people; learn from them. Bring all forces together to implement your goals. Be willing to adapt to the needs of the group, even if it seems to alter your vision. This is the time for organization.

Your roots are strong, so it is time to grow upward and seek the sun. Set your sights on ascending – on climbing the ladder in power and position. Gather your resources around you. Prepare well, as if you were going to climb an unknown mountain. Visualize possible problems, and solve them in your mind. This path requires careful preparation and concerted effort, but your time and work will be amply rewarded.

## 47. K'UN LAKE / WATER
## IMPRISONMENT

KEYWORDS
✦ anxiety ✦ restrictions ✦ fear ✦

LAKE

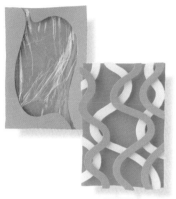

WATER

You are cut off from your sources of help and nourishment. Do not put your trust in the words of others, and do not expect your words to be believed. Speak little, do less, and wait for a more auspicious time to act. Trust yourself and your deepest held beliefs. Don't despair, this imprisonment will end soon.

## 48. CHING WATER / WIND
## THE WELL

KEYWORDS
✦ common resources ✦ nucleus ✦
✦ a well ✦

The source of inspiration and truth lies beneath you like a deep well, but you must dig deep into your nature to access it. Determine which truths you are certain of and live by, your sources of hope and inspiration. Once connected, maintain your access by consistently dipping into the well of your deepest truth.

## 49. KO LAKE / FIRE
### REVOLUTION

KEYWORDS
✦ elimination ✦ change ✦
✦ skinning an animal ✦

LAKE

FIRE

You can make huge strides forward by stripping away old patterns and choosing to express yourself in a new way. Boldly step forward as the self you have wanted to be. Put aside old disagreements and regrets. Observe your situation and wait for the right time to reveal a new you to everyone. Trust your instincts and you will be protected by the universal forces.

## 50. TING FIRE / WIND
### THE CALDRON

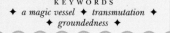

KEYWORDS
✦ a magic vessel ✦ transmutation ✦
✦ groundedness ✦

FIRE

WIND

Focus is the key to transformation of your situation. Refine your ideas, distill your efforts to their essence, then contain them in your mind. Once you have had time for reflection, you can bring the transforming power of positive vision to bear on your situation. Actively repicture it in its most positive light. Turn it over in your mind, until you have recreated every aspect. What your mind can contain in its magic caldron, you can create.

## 51. CHEN THUNDER / THUNDER
### SHOCK

> **KEYWORDS**
> ✦ *awakening* ✦ *breakthrough* ✦
> ✦ *an earthquake* ✦

This is the time when the judgment call resounds – are you frightened or joyful? This is a shocking period of huge changes. Don't lose your grounding, or cry for help as you see others do. Remain calm, unswerving in your purpose, for when the shock passes you will find gold at your feet.

## 52. KEN MOUNTAIN / MOUNTAIN
### STILLNESS

> **KEYWORDS**
> ✦ *boundary* ✦ *completion* ✦
> ✦ *standstill* ✦

You have reached the limit of this situation. You must still yourself to perceive the true nature of your condition. You cannot move forward from this point. Look beyond your current desires to a bigger picture. Recognize what has already been completed. Refrain from compulsive action. Rest.

## 53. **CHIEN** WIND / MOUNTAIN
## STEADY DEVELOPMENT

KEYWORDS
◆ *permeating* ◆ *flowing* ◆
◆ *drop by drop* ◆

## 54. **KUEI MEI** THUNDER / LAKE
## DESTINY

KEYWORDS
◆ *changing form* ◆ *belonging* ◆
◆ *a maiden about to wed* ◆

THUNDER

LAKE

Proceedings occur at a snail's pace, with slow, continual advancement. Do not be discouraged if you cannot perceive progress. Continue to move toward your goal step by step. Patience is necessary, but you are certain to achieve your desired outcome.

You are being led by a force greater than you are into a new situation. Passively accept what fate has put in your path. It is of untold benefit to you. It is unwise to argue, and you cannot escape the influence of fate on your present situation. Let go of any attachments to your present situation and prepare yourself for enormous change.

## 55. FENG THUNDER / FIRE
## PLENTY

KEYWORDS
♦ luxurious ♦ abundant ♦
♦ exuberant ♦

THUNDER

FIRE

This is your time to shine. Your enthusiasm and energy radiate to all around. Keep the flow of ideas and wealth open by sharing with others. Put arguments and misunderstandings behind you. Imagine you bring light to the world just by being who you really are – then act accordingly, and let your light shine.

## 56. LÜ FIRE / MOUNTAIN
## JOURNEYING

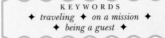

KEYWORDS
♦ traveling ♦ on a mission ♦
♦ being a guest ♦

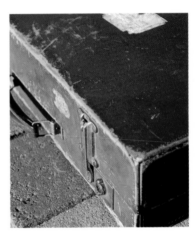

You cannot advance your cause by remaining where you are. Dismantle your present structures and venture out, seeking fertile ground for your desires. Travel light, scouting for the right people and places. Remain on the sidelines, observing. The adaptive lessons you learn on your journey are just the ones you need in order to move to the next level with your vision.

## 57. SUN WIND / WIND
### IMPRESSIONABLE

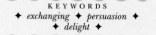

> KEYWORDS
> ✦ submissive ✦ supported ✦
> ✦ be shaped by ✦

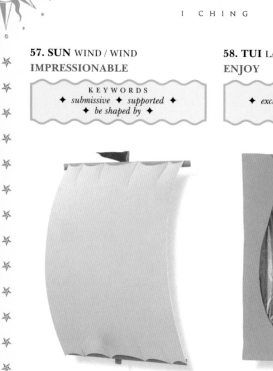

You've chosen a big issue to tackle, and your surest path is to infiltrate subtly. Allow yourself to be molded by the prevailing winds of the situation. Adapt to the higher powers at work, and in this way penetrate to the core of power. If you are firmly rooted to your goal, your impressionability will work for you.

## 58. TUI LAKE / LAKE
### ENJOY

> KEYWORDS
> ✦ exchanging ✦ persuasion ✦
> ✦ delight ✦

It's party time! Socializing, gathering friends together, encouraging play and good humor will bring you joy and higher rewards. Be the enthusiastic host, and practice any creative activity that pleases you. This pleasant, fulfilling time opens channels of energy and opportunity in every direction.

## 59. HUAN WIND / WATER
### SCATTERING

KEYWORDS
✦ *wash away* ✦ *clear up* ✦ *disperse* ✦

WIND

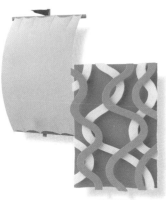

WATER

You may feel blocked, but don't hesitate in acting now. Clear up misunderstandings, dispel fears, and shine light on all your efforts. You have the support to achieve great things. Take the lead and be fluid and flexible in your path. Your actions will clear the blockage of energy, recharging you and everyone else involved.

## 60. CHIEH WATER / LAKE
### ORGANIZATION

KEYWORDS
✦ *sections* ✦ *economy* ✦ *limits* ✦

WATER

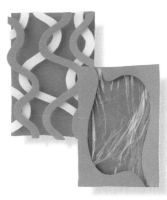

LAKE

Polish up your administrative skills, for it's the right time to reorganize, file, update your address book, and take care of unfinished business. Set a schedule and manage your time. This hexagram represents articulation and separation of ideas into constructive units. Use its power to reorganize your affairs.

### 61. CHUNG FU WIND / LAKE
### CONCORDANCE

> KEYWORDS
> ◆ inner stability ◆ reliability ◆
> ◆ sincerity ◆

### 62. HSIAO KUO THUNDER / MOUNTAIN
### SMALL DETAILS

> KEYWORDS
> ◆ little or unimportant ◆
> ◆ getting clear of ◆ lessen ◆

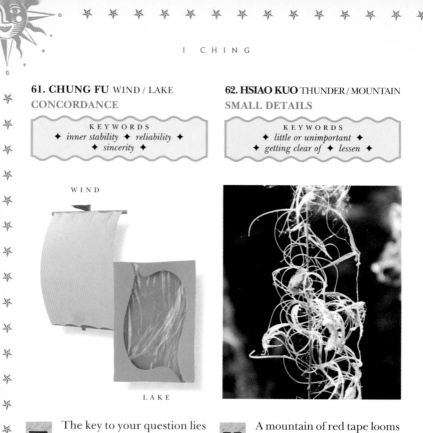

WIND

LAKE

The key to your question lies in your ability to make your actions fit your words and ideals. You will gain support only if you are practicing what you preach. If you can exhibit your trustworthiness, you will move forward quickly along your path. If you are facing obstacles, look within to find where your ideals and actions are not in accord.

A mountain of red tape looms on your horizon. Pay careful attention to the details of your situation, but don't get overwhelmed by them. Be conscientious and take care of one thing at a time. You are moving at a snail's pace toward your goal, but you are nevertheless moving. Keep your courage, set your eyes firmly on your goal, and get started!

## 63. CHI CHI WATER / FIRE
## IN THE MIDST

KEYWORDS
✦ crossing a river ✦ overcoming ✦
✦ a half-eaten meal ✦

You're well on your way to completion now, and everything is bubbling along. Resist the temptation to become complacent, and keep putting time and energy into your project. The universal flow is supporting you, but if you stop paddling, your boat will sink or run aground.

## 64. WEI CHI FIRE / WATER
## ON THE VERGE

KEYWORDS
✦ overcoming ✦ beginning ✦
✦ has not yet occurred ✦

FIRE

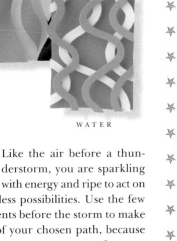

WATER

Like the air before a thunderstorm, you are sparkling with energy and ripe to act on countless possibilities. Use the few moments before the storm to make sure of your chosen path, because the soon-to-come surge of energy will whisk you quite a long way. Once you are sure of your direction, fasten your seat belt and set off on a new adventure.

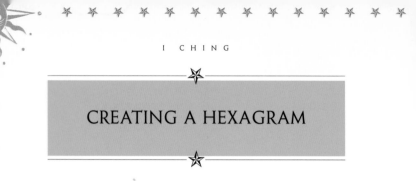

# CREATING A HEXAGRAM

*The traditional way to consult the I Ching is by drawing from a bunch of yarrow stalks. However, a much simpler and equally reliable method is to throw three identical coins. To generate your hexagram you must first formulate a clear and concise question for the oracle.*

First, frame your question. Think carefully about this and phrase it to avoid any ambiguity. Write it down.

Take any three identical coins, shake them well in your cupped hands, and toss them onto a flat surface. Each throw creates one line of the hexagram and starts from the bottom, working its way to the top.

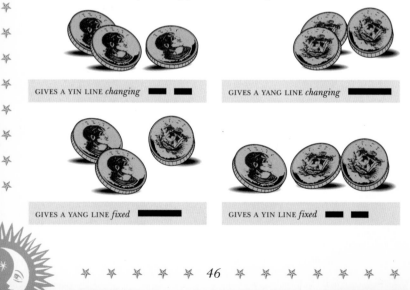

GIVES A YIN LINE *changing* ▬▬ ▬▬

GIVES A YANG LINE *changing* ▬▬▬▬▬

GIVES A YANG LINE *fixed* ▬▬▬▬▬

GIVES A YIN LINE *fixed* ▬▬ ▬▬

Throw the coins a second time to create the second line and so on until you have six lines, stacking one on top of another.

Your finished hexagram might look like this.

SIXTH THROW *3 tails*

FIFTH THROW *3 heads*

FOURTH THROW *2 heads, 1 tail*

THIRD THROW *2 heads, 1 tail*

SECOND THROW *3 tails*

FIRST THROW *2 tails, 1 head*

Some lines are considered to be so charged with positive or negative energy that they can move or change into their opposite. If you have a "changing" line (three heads or three tails), mark it as (1) for three heads and (2) for three tails.

Changing lines in this hexagram would look like the following.

The changing lines are transforming into their opposites, broken line becoming complete line, yin turning into yang, and vice versa.

Redraw the hexagram and it now looks like the one above. This is your second hexagram, which gives the potential outcome to your question. The first hexagram is your present situation, the second tells you what is likely to happen in your life if you follow the advice of the first.

To identify your hexagram turn to the chart on page 54 and match the upper and lower trigrams.

## HOW TO INTERPRET THE HEXAGRAMS

The hexagrams shown here and interpreted are examples of the kind of answers you will receive and the way you should try to interpret them. Don't be surprised if the response is puzzling in some cases. Carry the images in your mind for a day or two, perhaps a week or more, until they come into focus. The process of interpretation is made easier if you keep your questions simple and direct.

### QUESTION
Shall I change my job?

### ANSWER
Hexagram 9
**HSIAO CH'U**
Small Gathering
*Changing to*
Hexagram 55
**FENG** Plenty

Do not seek employment elsewhere at the moment. In this case, Hexagram 9 advises you to tolerate your present employment because your actual situation is invisible to you. It will change of its own accord to Plenty. The answer could also have been:

Hexagram 56
**LÜ** Journeying
*Changing to*
Hexagram 55
**FENG** Plenty

Hexagram 56 suggests movement but be aware of a literal interpretation. Stay in touch with your inner voice and allow intuition to reveal the true meaning of Journeying.

### QUESTION
Shall I take a vacation in China?

### ANSWER
Hexagram 21
**SHIH HO** Gnawing
*Changing to*
Hexagram 50
**TING** The Caldron

Yes, now is the time to visit this exciting country. China is a magic caldron for you but there are obstacles to overcome. Gnaw at them and bite your way through. Another answer might be:

Hexagram 24
**FU** Return
*Changing to*
Hexagram 25
**WU WANG** Disentangling

Hexagram 24 advises a return to source and 25 suggests rashness, recklessness, and negative emotion. Perhaps the time is not right. Disentangle your life at home first.

## QUESTION
Shall I invite the new guy in my office to a movie?

## ANSWER
Hexagram 10
**LÜ** Treading
*Changing to*
Hexagram 58
**TUI** Enjoy

Hexagram 10 says you should take one step at a time that will lead you to Hexagram 58, Enjoy! However, the I Ching might have counseled against looking for a new relationship here. Changing lines in the first and second positions would have given the following:

Hexagram 10
**LÜ** Treading
*Changing to*
Hexagram 12
**PI** Obstruction

Taking one step at a time will only lead you to an obstruction. Better forget it.

## QUESTION
Shall I end the relationship with my partner?

## ANSWER
Hexagram 27
**YI** Nourishment
*Changing to*
Hexagram 11
**T'AI** Peaceful Flow

Hexagram 27 asks if you are nourishing yourself as well as others. Do so, and you will find peace. However tempted we are to resolve relationships, the I Ching invariably recommends patience and quiet maturity. But the same question might just as easily have elicited this response:

Hexagram 6
**SUNG** Conflict
*Changing to*
Hexagram 38
**K'UEI** Separation

Are you picking fights with your partner? You risk separation, from him or her and the Tao (your destiny) if you continue this way. But seek also deeper meanings, with conflict and separation as figurative energies within yourself.

I CHING

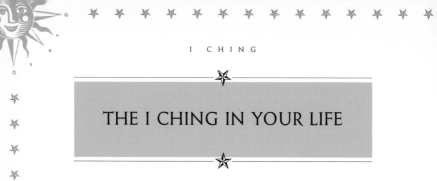

# THE I CHING IN YOUR LIFE

*In many systems of divination, the process of consulting the oracle is called a reading. You may have heard people speak of palm reading or tarot reading. In the I Ching, a reading would include asking the question, building the hexagram, and interpreting the result.*

USE ANY THREE IDENTICAL COINS
TO READ THE I CHING ORACLE.

## DOING A READING

The majority of the hexagrams are straightforward and can easily be applied to many kinds of situations. There are times, however, when the relationship between the hexagram and the question is unclear. If you are having trouble applying the hexagram to your situation or emotional state of mind, then go back to your question. Reread it for clarity and completeness. Apply the hexagram's meaning back to the specific wording of your question. Can you break down the question or simplify it in any way? If so, rephrase your inquiry and ask again.

You might decide to delve further into the issues by asking even more specific questions in order to probe areas that seem obscure or inconsistent.

You can also use the oracle to ask your own questions about other people's lives and problems. However, any reading you do about other people without their knowledge and consent provides information that should be kept strictly to yourself. Do not inform them of the reading and its outcome. It is possible that the information you receive is the state of their situation *as it concerns you*. They might obtain a very different response were they to throw the coins themselves. If you wish to share information about another that you have obtained in a reading, first tell the person that you were inquiring into their situation using the I Ching. Then, if they are interested and if they wish to hear more, explain to them the specific question and its outcome. Better yet, invite them to do their own reading with you!

*Ask as many questions as you like – but be aware of overasking the same question, or working too long at one sitting. Sometimes the meaning of the hexagram will become clear over time. Try again after a few days.*

*Use caution in sharing your findings and experiences of the hexagrams with others. Don't allow their input to influence your understanding of a situation – especially if they are suspicious or negative about a particular situation.*

## INTUITION AND
## PERSONAL RESPONSIBILITY

周易 The strength of any oracle lies in its ability to help seekers uncover the truths within themselves. The poetry of the hexagrams refers to one state of energy on its path of constant transformation. Though the state referred to in the hexagram is specific, it need not be taken literally at all times. Your own intuition should be nurtured and increasingly relied upon when consulting the I Ching. By developing your intuitive powers, you will start working with the I Ching on a much deeper level. You can begin to sense and observe the movement of the Tao through your life situations even *before* you consult the oracle.

Practice sharpening your intuition by familiarizing yourself with all 64 hexagrams. Notice the cycles of yielding and asserting, obstacles and breakthroughs that make up the I Ching. Then, before you build your hexagram, ask a question and play at answering it yourself, using your knowledge of the hexagrams as a guide. Assess the situation as to the life energy at work and from a wider perspective.

Now, throw the coins and consult the oracle. Even if the oracle gives you very different information, you will have achieved greater inner clarity before consulting the I Ching. Don't get discouraged or dismiss the oracle if your intuition and the hexagram say differing things. Remember that this is not a test, but an information gathering process.

*For a quick reading of the oracle (or for intuition practice), simply close your eyes, think of your question, and open the book at a hexagram. Read the first hexagram that your eyes fall on. If you open at something other than a hexagram, simply close the book and try the process again.*

*The I Ching was meant to advise and help, but not to govern. Use it wisely to nurture your own insights and intuitions. If you find yourself losing confidence in your ability to make decisions without first consulting the oracle, then think about putting it away for a while. Alternatively try using the techniques for increasing your intuitive powers. The answers to your questions are, and always have been, within yourself.*

## DOING READINGS
## FOR OTHER PEOPLE

周易 There are many ways of using the I Ching to work with others and it is a great test of your clarity and understanding of it. Act as a medium for your friend and help them frame a clear question. Hold their question in your mind while you throw the coins and build the hexagram. Share the meaning of the hexagram with the other person and offer support if they are disappointed by the outcome of the reading. If necessary, help them to formulate other questions to gain greater insight into their situation.

Instruct someone to do a reading themselves: act as a guide, helping to clarify the question, build the hexagram, and interpret its advice. Offer suggestions for other questions to put to the oracle, which would probe the issues more deeply.

*It's easy to do readings over the phone! Simply proceed as if the person were present. The questioner asks the question, you throw the coins and read the result. You can also try it over the Internet on a chat line.*

## KEEPING A JOURNAL

周易 Try keeping a journal to record your experience with the I Ching. By making a note of the date, your question, the hexagram, and any insights or ideas about how it applies to your query, you will begin to see how the hexagram reflects the inner truth of your predicament. You might find that a certain hexagram figures prominently in your life, even though it is formed in response to entirely different questions.

*Keeping a record of your readings will encourage you to develop an intuitive understanding of the hexagrams. Familiarity with a hexagram and how it applied in the past will help you to interpret its link to your current predicament far more quickly. Using a journal will also help you to clarify problems and focus your ideas into a searching question; and by recording the evolution of an issue or situation, you will gain a greater insight into the Tao.*
*Decorate your journal with beautiful colors and inspiring designs. Use a special pen to record your reading, or experiment with colored inks or pencils.*

# HOW TO FIND YOUR HEXAGRAM

*Match the upper and lower trigrams in order to find your hexagram.*

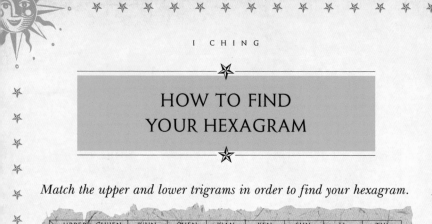

| UPPER / LOWER | CH'IEN Heaven | K'UN Earth | CHEN Thunder | K'AN Water | KEN Mountain | SUN Wind | LI Fire | TUI Lake |
|---|---|---|---|---|---|---|---|---|
| CH'IEN Heaven | 1 | 11 | 34 | 5 | 26 | 9 | 14 | 43 |
| K'UN Earth | 12 | 2 | 16 | 8 | 23 | 20 | 35 | 45 |
| CHEN Thunder | 25 | 24 | 51 | 3 | 27 | 42 | 21 | 17 |
| K'AN Water | 6 | 7 | 40 | 29 | 4 | 59 | 64 | 47 |
| KEN Mountain | 33 | 15 | 62 | 39 | 52 | 53 | 56 | 31 |
| SUN Wind | 44 | 46 | 32 | 48 | 18 | 57 | 50 | 28 |
| LI Fire | 13 | 36 | 55 | 63 | 22 | 37 | 30 | 49 |
| TUI Lake | 10 | 19 | 54 | 60 | 41 | 61 | 38 | 58 |

CHINESE PHILOSOPHER AND TEACHER, CONFUCIUS,
MEETING LAO TSU, FOUNDER OF TAOISM.

## FURTHER READING

CLEARY, Thomas, trans.,
*The Secret of the Golden Flower*
(HarperCollins, San Francisco,
1991)

HIEDER, John, *The Tao of Leadership*
(Humanics, Atlanta, 1985)

HUANG, Kerson and Rosemary,
*I Ching* (Workman, New York, 1985)

KARCHER, Stephen,
*The Elements of the I Ching*
(Element, Shaftesbury, 1995)

KARCHER, Stephen, *The Illustrated
Encyclopedia of Divination*
(Element, Shaftesbury, 1997)

PALMER, Martin,
*The Elements of Taoism*,
(Element, Shaftesbury, 1995)

RITSEMA, Rudolf and KARCHER,
Stephen, *I Ching: The Classic
Chinese Oracle of Change*
(Element, Shaftesbury, 1994)

WILHELM, Richard and BAYNES,
Cary F., *The I Ching, or Book of
Changes* (Princeton University
Press, Princeton, 1967)

WING, R., *The I Ching Workbook*
(Doubleday, New York, 1982)

WONG, Eva, *The Shambhala
Guide to Taoism* (Shambhala,
Boston, 1997)

# INDEX